THE
BLUFFER'S GUIDE
TO
CRICKET

NICK YAPP

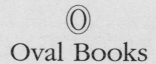

Oval Books

Published by Oval Books
335 Kennington Road
London SE11 4QE

Telephone: (0171) 582 7123
Fax: (0171) 582 1022
E-mail: info@ovalbooks.com

First published by Ravette Publishing.
This edition published by Oval Books.

First edition 1988
Updated 1991, 1992, 1993, 1995
Reprinted 1996
Updated 1997, 1998
New edition 1999

Series Editor – Anne Tauté

Cover designer – Jim Wire, Quantum
Printer – Caledonian International Ltd

The Bluffer's Guides® series is based
on an original idea by Peter Wolfe.

CONTENTS

Note: 'Batsman' embraces batswoman – but never in front of, and only rarely behind, the sightscreen.

INTRODUCTION

It has been said that the English, not being by nature a religious people, invented cricket to give them some idea of Eternity. This is blatant bluff, though it does indicate that cricket is not to be treated lightly or dismissed as merely a sport.

The English did not invent cricket, but they acted as its wet nurse, they nurtured it, and finally made it their own. This is because cricket needs endless patience, unthinking loyalty, a slavish mentality: not the sort of game you can see being enjoyed by the hordes of Genghis Khan, or the Sioux, or the Paris mob of 1789, or the Bolsheviks. G. M. Trevelyan (famous historian and useful late order bat) once suggested that, if the aristocracy of L'Ancien Régime had spent more time playing cricket with their serfs, the French Revolution would never have taken place. The truth is that neither the French aristocracy nor their serfs could ever have wanted to play cricket – it is not their game.

Bored almost beyond endurance, the uninitiated, watching or even playing cricket, will moan: 'What's the point of it?' Bluffers know that there is no point to cricket (although there is a cover point) any more than there is a point to tennis, ballet, rose gardens or nouvelle cuisine. Cricket maintains its precarious existence because the show must go on. It has to be shown that people can:

a) bowl faster
b) score more runs
c) make more appearances for their county
d) take longer to score a run than ever before.

This, you must maintain stoutly (cricketers do lots of things stoutly) provides proof of human progress.

ORIGINS

Like the cricket field, the field of cricket is ripe for bluffers – no one even knows the origin of the word 'cricket', let alone the game, but it seems to be derived from either the Anglo-Saxon 'cricce', the French 'criquet' or the Dutch 'krickstoel'.

A cricce was a staff or crutch. In the Bodleian Library, there is a picture of medieval monks standing in a field, one brother bowling to another who is attempting to hit the ball with his cricce. Instead of a wicket there is a hole in the ground. This is reckoned by experts to be a very early form of the game 'clubball', forerunner of cricket. But it could simply be a picture of some medieval monks being silly in a field.

There are references in 15th century French literature to 'criquet' (it was played at St Omer as soon as they'd got over the Hundred Years War), and in an Italian dictionary of the 16th century there is reference to 'cricket-a-wicket'. This cosmopolitan scattering of information is perfect for bluffing purposes. You can wax lyrical over why it never caught on in Italy – imagine fielding at cover after a dish of pasta – and speculate wildly about the game's simultaneous development in Denmark, Holland, Germany and Persia (where it was called 'kruitskaukan'). There is probably a picture in Tehran University of a group of ayatollahs being silly in a field.

In 1613 Oliver Cromwell is said to have thrown himself into a 'dissolute and disorderly course' by playing cricket – there's depravity. In 1676 a party of British sailors played cricket in Aleppo. What they were doing in Syria, some 80 miles inland, when they were supposed to have been fighting the Dutch in the Medway isn't explained, but may be evidence of the early importance attached to cricket in terms of international prestige.

The Marylebone Cricket Club

The Headquarters of the MCC is at Lords in a posh part of London called St John's Wood. It was founded in 1787 by ex-patrons of the Hambledon Club, which up to then regarded itself as the controller of the game. Hambledon fell into a decline, which was perhaps as well, or the BBC would have to lug all their heavy television cameras out to Broadha'penny Down whenever a Cup Final was played.

It is considered something of an honour to be a member of the MCC, or so members of the MCC say. There is a waiting list of several thousand, and you have to show that you wear a suit, stiff collar and tie *at all times*, treat women like ladies, know your way round a decent wine list, and can go to sleep on a hard seat in the open air.

The MCC is the custodian of cricket. It has a museum of the game, a collection of books, more memorabilia than it has room for, and it pronounces on the rights and wrongs of cricket in general. Because it is London based, it is viewed with great suspicion by all the County clubs except Middlesex, who share Lords with the MCC and are consequently given preferential treatment. The bright bluffer knows that this is why Middlesex play all their Cup Finals on their home ground, and why there have been more captains of England from Middlesex than any other county.

The MCC and Lords is hated most of all by Surrey fans, because:

a) Lords is north of the river, and Surrey's ground (The Oval) is south of the river.
b) No recognition is given to the fact that, historically, far more important matches have been played, and decisions about cricket taken, at The Oval.
c) The MCC talks proper and Surrey talks common.

The Ashes

In a match that lasted only two days (28th and 29th August, 1882), Australia beat England for the first time in England. One spectator dropped dead and another bit chunks out of his umbrella handle (Augusts were soaking wet too, a hundred years ago). The next day, *The Sporting Times* published its famous mock obituary:

> 'In affectionate Remembrance of
> English Cricket
> which died at The Oval, 29th August, 1882,
> deeply lamented by a large circle of sorrowing
> friends and acquaintances. R.I.P.
> N.B. The body will be cremated and
> the ashes taken to Australia.'

The following winter England beat Australia in Australia, and some Melbourne ladies burnt a bail, sealed the ashes in an urn, and inscribed the urn with a rather sweet little poem that included the couplet:

> 'The welkin will ring loud,
> The great crowd will feel proud...'

Australians have always been better at cricket than poetry. The ladies presented the urn to the English captain, the Hon. Ivo Bligh, and one of them subsequently married him. When the Hon. Ivo died, he bequeathed the Ashes to the MCC. Since 1927 they have remained at Lords, even though England did not win them once between 1934 and 1953.

Nowadays, Test series between England and Australia are played for other trophies and lots and lots of lovely prize money, but the fate of the Ashes still matters much to men with striped ties and watery eyes.

The Bodyline Tour

Half a century ago it was all very different. The Ashes mattered enormously to everyone. National pride was at stake. In 1930 Australia had beaten England in England. Normally, a gunboat would have been dispatched to shell Sydney Harbour, but, instead, in the winter of 1932-3, Douglas Jardine was sent to Australia with a team that included three very fast bowlers: Larwood, Voce and Bowes. Everybody seems roughly agreed on what happened, but there are different versions as to how it happened and why it happened.

The Boys Own Paper Theory suggests that Jardine was a jolly good Public School chap who understandably found it hard to talk to the colonials when they squeaked about being hit on the head and heart by a hard ball propelled at speeds in excess of 90 miles per hour.

The Establishment Theory is that the whole thing was badly handled, and would have been sorted out in ten seconds pronto by the autocratic Lord Harris of Seringapatam and Mysore and Belmont (who must have been a pretty smart fellow, being Lord of three places so far apart) if his Lordship had not made the mistake of dying the previous spring.

The Professional Cricketers' Theory is that they had to do as they were told by the Amateur Captain.

The TV Drama Theory is that Childhood Rejection + Fanatical Will to Win + Stiff Upper Lip + Bright Eyed Kid from the Outback + Bunch of Bronzed Blokes Showing Off their Physical Skills + Couple of Near Lethal Injuries = Good Viewing Figures.

The Oz School of Journalism Theory suggests that the Whingeing Poms were so scared of Bradman, who had averaged around 150 runs per innings in the 1930 Test Series, that they resorted to desperate, nay criminal, nay warlike, measures to get him out.

For the Bodyline Theory was very simple. You simply placed a cordon of fielders near the wicket on the leg side (see Glossary), and bowled at the batsman's body.

The Australians were incensed. Their Board of Control sent an alarmist cable to the MCC. The MCC Committee met to discuss it. At that time, the Committee consisted of:

6 Peers
5 Knights
The Speaker of the House of Commons
The Chairman of the Unionist Party
An ex-Governor of Bengal
A Cabinet Minister
A Lord Mayor of London
6 cricketers (what they were doing there, goodness only knows)

So the Committee clearly had its ear to the ground, knew what the man-in-the-street was thinking, finger on the pulse of democracy, etc.

In the end the whole thing blew over. More cables were sent. A couple of England players were set up as sacrifices. The Australian crowds were condemned for barracking at the matches where their players were injured. More significantly, the Laws were modified to outlaw Bodyline bowling. Today umpires are empowered to warn a bowler whom they consider is deliberately intimidating a batsman. If the bowler does not heed the warning, the umpires can instruct the captain that s/he may bowl no more in that innings. And restrictions were placed on the number of fielders you could put close to the wicket on the leg side.

Australia is still a member of the Commonwealth.

WHAT HAPPENS IN CRICKET

Those unfamiliar with the game should read this section very slowly, several times, and in a charitable frame of mind.

Cricket is about **scoring runs** and **taking wickets**. In most matches, the side that scores the greater number of runs, wins (for exceptions see next section).

Perhaps the simplest way to explain cricket is to describe what happens.

1. A field is mown. A 'square' in the middle is mown even shorter. A 'pitch' on the square is mown shortest of all, so that there isn't any grass left.
2. Two white 'creases' are painted at each end of the pitch. They mark the areas from which a bowler may safely bowl, and in which a batsman may safely stand.
3. Three sticks, called 'stumps', are tapped into the ground at each end of the pitch. Any boy using the face of the bat to knock the stumps in, is caned.
4. Two fat umpires waddle out. They place little bridging pieces of wood, called 'bails' on both sets of stumps.
5. The umpires throw a ball to and fro, to show what lads they once were.

All this activity, and the game hasn't even started yet.

6. The fielding side come out of the pavilion, wiping their mouths and feigning physical fitness. The Captain leads, followed by minor members of the aristocracy, ordained ministers, and, last of all, sweaty but honest professionals.
7. Two batsmen emerge, pale but proud. The 'non-striker' stands by the bowler's wicket. The 'striker' stands by the other wicket.

11

8. One fat umpire throws the ball to the bowler and shouts 'Play!'
9. It starts to rain. The bowler runs up and hurls the ball at the striker, or the wicket, or somewhere roughly in that direction.
10. After six such hurls (an 'over') the bowling switches to the other end and somebody else has a go.

From this point onwards, it is a matter of the batsmen getting as many runs as possible, and the bowlers and fielders getting them out. This is effected as follows:

Bowled – The batsman hits or misses the ball, which travels on and knocks a bail off the stumps.

Caught – The batsman hits the ball which is grabbed by the fielder or bowler before it hits the ground.

Stumped – The batsman misses the ball. The wicket keeper catches the ball. The batsman foolishly leaves 'safe' ground. The wicket keeper removes a bail by striking the stumps with the hand in which the ball is held.

Run Out – The batsman hits or misses the ball. Tries to run from one end of the pitch to the other, or leaves the crease and tries to get back, but before regaining safe ground, the fielder either throws the ball to the bowler or wicket keeper (who do as in stumped) or throws the ball directly on to the wicket, knocking a bail off.

Hit Wicket – While trying to hit the ball, the batsman hits his own wicket. The hara-kiri of cricket.

Leg Before Wicket (LBW) – Diabolically hard to understand, but something to do with ball hitting the batsman's leg when it would otherwise have hit the wicket. Do not bother about the details as the law changes as often as Trade Union legislation. LBW is a desperate attempt to bring controversy to a game stifled with unanimity of opinion.

There are three other ways to be 'out' – **Handled The Ball**, **Hit The Ball Twice**, and **Obstructed The Field**. It should be clear from their titles what they entail, and that they apply only to absolute bounders.

Some bowlers believe the best way to dismiss a batsman is by crippling him or her. (See The Bodyline Tour.) Since there have to be two batsman available at any time, a complete side of eleven is dismissed when ten wickets have fallen or ten batsmen have been crippled.

Appeals

Sometimes it is obvious when a batsman is dismissed. The stumps may be spread-eagled or the ball clearly caught. Besides, the batsman's upper lip stiffens while the lower quivers. But often there is room for doubt. It is here that the 'appeal' comes into play. In theory, one of the fielding side has to say 'How was that?', and the umpire has to respond either by indicating that the batsman is out or by *saying* that the batsman isn't.

In practice, the bowler and as many fielders as are still awake scream a monosyllabic 'Zzhhaarrtt!', and the umpire either indicates out (see Umpires) or snorts contemptuously. It is not unknown for modern cricketers to disagree with the umpire and display anguish if their appeal is disallowed. This display may take the form of spitting, punching the ground, twisting the features of the face into an ugly pattern, or, apparently, mouthing the word 'flip!'.

Making Runs

There are two ways of making runs:

1. The batsman hits the ball out of the field of play (6 runs without bouncing, 4 runs with). This is called a boundary and spectators are expected to wake up and clap.

2. The batsman hits the ball far enough for both batsmen to change ends. This can be exciting, since each has to judge the safety of his or her position. It often leads to the following sort of verbal exchange:

> *Striker*: Yes!
> *Non Striker*: Wait!
> *Striker*: (who will be credited with the run if they make it) Come on!
> *Non Striker*: No!!
> *Striker*: (now several strides down the wicket) Run, you fool!
> *Non Striker*: (damned if he or she is risking being out for another's run) Get back!
> *Striker:* (damned if he or she is going back) Come ON!!
> *Non Striker*: ****!!

By now, both batsmen are at the same end of the pitch, looking very silly and hating each other. At the other end, the fielding side have removed the bails and are covering their mouths with their hands to smother sniggers. One of the batsmen is out. Which? Probably the non-striker, the more passive of the two, although the Laws of Cricket would say otherwise.

Either way, one batsman has to make the supreme sacrifice, and walk back to the pavilion, a white flannelled Sidney Carton. Vast sympathy awaits. Cricket is flooded with sympathy. Sympathy for being out, for having been given out when you weren't, for letting the ball pass between your feet and looking foolish, for bowling all afternoon and not taking a single wicket, for not getting a chance to bowl, for bowling a load of tripe and being hit all over the park, for scoring no runs, for scoring 99 runs, for not getting a chance to bat, for dropping eight simple catches. The more inept the performance, the greater the sympathy.

The other way runs are scored is called **extras**. These consist of:

Bye – The batsman misses the ball, so does the wicket keeper. Everyone looks foolish. The batsmen change ends.

Leg Bye – The ball, not in line with the wicket (otherwise LBW), hits the batsman's leg or body. Bounces far enough away for the batsmen to change ends.

No Ball – When the bowler oversteps the crease while delivering the ball. The umpire is supposed to shout 'N' ba'!!' and to stick an arm out sideways so the batsman knows he may take a mighty swing at the ball, since the only way you can be out off a no ball is 'run out'.

Wide – The ball is bowled so wide of the wicket that a batsman could not be reasonably expected to hit it, even if so desirous.

At the end of a team's innings, the total number of runs is totted up. The other team has to get at least one run more before losing ten wickets. If both teams score the same number of runs, the side losing fewer wickets wins. If both sides score the same number of runs and lose the same number of wickets, it is a 'tie'. In Test and County cricket, there is one other possible end – a draw.

Fielding Positions

Never call anyone a 'backstop'. There is no such position in cricket, and it shows you to be a complete duffer, not bluffer, fit only for softball or rounders. There is, however, a 'longstop' but this position is only occupied when the fielding side has an appallingly bad wicket keeper. Since it is considered a disgrace to need a longstop, what you do is put someone in the longstop position, but call them 'very fine leg'.

In the days of the Bodleian picture of monks being silly, there were no set positions. People stood where they liked. Though the uninitiated may think the same holds true today, fielding positions have been scientifically established over the last 200 years as being *those places where the ball is most likely to be hit.*

Attacking Field

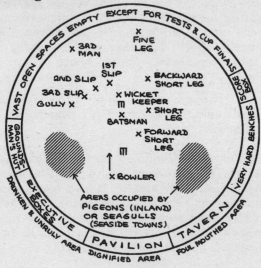

Sadly, there are not enough fielders to go everywhere the ball is most likely to be hit, so the Captain, in consultation with the bowler and the team's nosey parker, decides which nine gaps he will attempt to plug. At the beginning of an innings, when the bowler has a bright, shiny, hard, new ball and the batsmen are unsure and haven't got their eyes in, the Captain will set what is called an 'attacking' field. This means that most of the fielders are behind the batsman, looking menacingly at the bowler.

Once the shine has gone from the ball, the batsmen are well set and the bowlers are tired, the Captain will set a 'defensive' field. This means all the fielders are behind the bowler, looking menacingly at the batsman.

Defensive Field

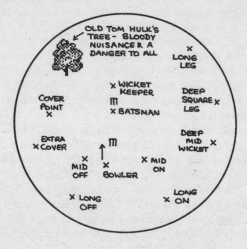

In general, you can put your fielders where you like, but there are some rules and restrictions (see The Bodyline Tour). Fast bowlers like to put all their fielders near the batsman. This is because fast bowlers rely on brute strength and do not expect a batsman to do more than defend. Slow bowlers like to put all their fielders as far away from the batsman as possible. This is because slow bowlers rely on guile and cunning, and expect the batsman will thrash their bowling all over the place. There is probably a deep truth about the human condition here. There are deep truths about the human condition throughout cricket.

Bluffers should avoid cricketing clichés, one of the worst of which is: 'It's fielders who win matches'. In school or club cricket this is meant to stiffen the resolve of those who are rotten batsmen or bowlers and are only in the team to make up the numbers. At County or International level, however, it approaches the truth. One dropped catch can cost a match: one brilliant 'run out' may save a match. And some of the greatest sights in cricket are those of really good fielders racing across the grass, swooping to pick up the ball on the run, then throwing it to the wicket-keeper with the speed and accuracy of a well aimed bullet. It only looks awful if it goes wrong.

In the old days, fielding was regarded as a chore. Batting and bowling were what mattered. You didn't get your name in the paper for running after a ball that someone else had hit off someone else's bowling. 'Lithe', 'supple', 'lissom' were not words generally applied to W.G. Grace, Alfred Mynn, or Lumpy Stevens (q.v.). Only 25 years ago, it was regular practice to stick out a large boot to stop the ball, and only the eccentric or show-offs would dive, even for a catch.

Nowadays fielders are expected to throw themselves upwards, downwards, sideways, even if it means permanent physical damage. A lot of cricket coaching has to do

18

with over-riding the natural self-protective instincts.

The Laws of Cricket

The present Laws are still roughly those laid down by Sir William Draper, His Grace the Duke of Dorset and their boozy chums on a night in February, 1774. There are 42 Laws in all, many with several clauses and sub-clauses. They cover substitutes; time-wasting; umpires; the rolling, sweeping, mowing, watering and marking of the pitch; the tea interval; dead balls; and unfair play, which includes 'lifting the seam', 'incommoding the striker' and unfairly 'stealing a run'. They are very soberly written, much venerated and occupy over thirty pages of very small print.

Cricket has Laws, not rules. There is, however, no system of appeal to the House of Lords, far less to the Court of Human Rights. You have to rely on the umpires.

Umpires

The duties of Umpires in cricket are as follows:

1. To make sure play starts on time.
2. To make sure the fielding side do not cheat by having too many people in their team or placing them illegally in the field.
3. To shout 'play' so that a match can begin.
4. To count up to six and then shout 'Over!'
5. To make sure the bowler does not bowl a no ball.
6. To hold the bowler's sweater while s/he bowls.
7. To make sure the batsman covers the full length of the pitch for a run.
8. To signal byes, wides, boundaries etc. to the scorers.

9. To check that the light is good enough for cricket. It is only in the last couple of years that umpires have been equipped with light meters to do this. Previously they had to rely on their own judgement, and their individual eyesight, and were to be seen on many a grey English evening, squinting at the clouds, and trying to imagine what it would be like to be young and have good eyes and be facing a fast bowler running in with a dark pavilion in the background.
10. To make sure that each session of play ends promptly.
11. To adjudicate whenever bowler and/or fielders appeal for a catch, stumping, LBW, run out, etc.

Since umpires are all aged, the hurly-burly of a run out is too much for them, so, for important matches, a Third Umpire is added. The Third Umpire's job is to sit in a warm room in the pavilion, watching television. When there is an appeal for a run out, the Third Umpire is awakened and his attention is directed to a video replay of what has happened. He then decides the outcome of the appeal – which everyone watching on television already knows.

In County and Test cricket, the umpire's role calls for fine judgement and complete impartiality, together with the ability to appease a volatile and partisan crowd. The umpire signals that a batsman is out by raising the index finger of the right hand. In Australia, umpires raise their right arm as well, as though needing to go to the gents.

Sadly, bowlers and fielders are not beyond appealing when they know the batsman isn't out at all. There is a feeling that if you shout loud enough, often enough, the umpire will have to submit, sooner or later. In the meantime, fury builds up in the free seats, where 20 or so disgruntled wags decide to give the umpire a hard time, mockingly calling, thus: 'You're blind!' 'Put your specs on!' 'What's the matter? Got cramp in yer finger?' This last may be followed by ribald speculation as to how such an odd medical condition could have occurred.

Umpires do not join in such levity – they are weighed down with dignity, sweaters, spare balls and little stones with which they count the deliveries in each over.

Scoring

In the old days, all you needed to keep the score at a cricket match was a stick and a sharp knife. Each time a run was scored, you cut a notch on your stick. Now you need a computer. This is because of cricket's obsession with statistics. Each time a run is scored the following information must be recorded and be instantly available:

1. Team score.
2. Individual batsman's score.
3. Number of runs hit off bowler.
4. Run rate per over.
5. Strike rate of bowler per hundred balls.
6. Strike rate of batsman per hundred balls.
7. Run rate required per over by batting side.
8. Batsman's and bowler's overall averages for this year.
9. Batsman's and bowler's averages since they were born.
10. Number of times batsman has hit ball in *that* direction.
11. How long since batsman last did that.
12. How long since bowler last did that. Etc., etc., etc.

It's a bit like the BBC and ITV on Election Night: too many statistics chasing too little action equals a strong inducement to sleep.

But, should you go to a cricket match, you will see males of all ages, assiduously keeping score. Every time the bowler bowls, a dot (no run), a '1' (one run), '2', '3', '4', '6', 'x' (wide), '0' (no ball), 'w' (wicket) is recorded – against batsman's and bowler's names. And the total score is continuously marked. If a wicket falls, the following details are recorded:

a)   How the batsman was out.
b)   Who the bowler was.
c)   How many runs the batsman got.
d)   Team score when the wicket fell.
e)   The time when the wicket fell.

Always make the point that such persistent monitoring by spectators does not exist in any other sport. You do not see people at Wimbledon, Wentworth or Wembley carrying out similar functions for tennis, golf and football. It is as if nobody trusted anybody at cricket.

There are many theories as to why people should go to such trouble and expense. One theory is that, historically, much money depended on the outcome of games, and spectators liked to keep a check for themselves. Another theory is that it gives spectators something to do and prevents atrophy of the brain cells during bouts of play.

At important cricket matches, the scorers – one for each team – sit in a little box of their own, acknowledging the umpires' signals, and keeping very neat records. In club matches, everybody has to take a turn with the scorebook, which becomes increasingly untidy. In municipal cricket matches they cut notches on sticks with sharp knives.

KINDS OF CRICKET

For the true bluffer, a little knowledge is a useful thing so you need to know the different kinds of cricket that you may be required to feign an interest in.

Test Matches

This is the top level of cricket, and always the slowest. Matches last for up to six days, but it seems much longer. Often there is no positive result, and the games can be mind bogglingly boring (MBB). Test matches are those played between any two of these countries:

England	**Australia**	**New Zealand**
Pakistan	**India**	**Sri Lanka**
West Indies	**South Africa**	**Zimbabwe**

In India and Pakistan periods of paralytically slow cricket are enlivened by the occasional full scale riot. In the West Indies all is excitement, especially when stands collapse. In Manchester Test matches may last for only three days, two days, or one day, or no days at all. It depends how much it rains.

Test matches, like safe sex, come in what are called **Rubbers**. This means a series of up to six games. The aim of both captains is simply to stop the other team winning. You should point out that this is achieved by wasting time. Here's how it is done:

1. The bowler takes an excessively long run up, starting in the pavilion, racing through the tea room, down the steps (pausing only to open the little gate), across the field, etc.

2. The bowler then bowls too wide for the batsman (who also wants to waste time) to be bothered to hit it.

3. The bowler walks back to begin again, so slowly that each over may take up to a quarter of an hour.

4. The bowler keeps finding things wrong with the ball, his boots, a hamstring, the crowd, the wind, or the consistency of the turf.

5. The batsman pretends not to be ready when the bowler is into the last furlong of his run up. This is done by stepping briskly backwards from the crease, miming that something has flown into his eye. A great deal of time is thus wasted, especially if the bowler tries not to let go of the ball and consequently injures himself.

6. The batsman keeps finding things wrong with bat, his **box** (see Impedimenta), the light or the **sight-screen** (see Glossary). Unless the ball is straight he makes no attempt to hit it.

7. The fielders keep thinking they're not well. So they leave the field to have a little lie-down, or a massage, or a game of cards, or to put a bet on the outcome of the match. Substitutes have to be brought on, and more time is wasted telling them where to go and what to do.

To win a Test or County match, you have to score more runs than the other side *and dismiss them all twice*. This is why so many games end in a draw, neither side winning.

County Cricket

This is played between either First Class Counties (not necessarily those with Tory MPs) or Minor Counties (those with councils under LibDem control). Matches last four days, and are played in some of the loveliest towns in the country: Worksop, Uxbridge, Ebbw Vale, Basingstoke, Middlesborough and so forth.

There is an annual County Championship, which was always won by Yorkshire until Geoffrey Boycott came along.

One-Day Cricket

In 1963, Gillette had the bright idea of limiting county matches to only one day's play, and thereby putting an end to the aforementioned sloth-like ways of ensuring a draw. In one-day games, you either win or you jolly well lose.

One day games are called 'Limited Overs Cricket'. There are three sorts:

60 overs each side (formerly the Gillette Cup, now the Nat West Tournament);

55 overs each (Benson and Hedges Cup);

40 overs each (formerly John Player League and Refuge Assurance League, now AXA Equity and Law League).

All these tournaments attract far larger crowds than the four day games, but are said to be the ruination of English cricket by a) purists, b) traditionalists, c) selectors, d) commentators, and e) people living in counties that never win them. Note that nobody has asked the players what they think, but one-day cricket has only been in existence for some 35 years, so it's early days yet.

Overseas Cricket

All the major cricketing countries have their equivalents of county cricket:

Australia	–	Sheffield Shield
South Africa	–	Castle Currie Cup
West Indies	–	Red Stripe Cup
New Zealand	–	Shell Trophy
India	–	Ranji Trophy
Pakistan	–	Quaid-e-Azam Trophy
Sri Lanka	–	Donovan Andree Trophy
Zimbabwe	–	Logan Cup

Apart from this, overseas players are allowed to play in other countries during what would normally be their 'off' season. Each English county may play one overseas player at a time (another cause of the ruination of English cricket), generally a fast bowler. In return, English players fly south in the winter. This system confuses selectors, denies local talent, and delights spectators. For these reasons it may well be changed.

League Cricket

This is played in several northern counties, but the most famous is the Lancashire League. Small towns in Lancashire each employ one professional cricketer, often a player of international stature, who may be seeking domestic qualification to play for an English county. It sounds a bit like Gulliver among the Lilliputians, but Lancashire is a very tough cricketing county and has produced such heroes as A.C. Maclaren, whose 424 was for 99 years the highest individual score on an English ground; George Duckworth, who had the loudest appeal heard on an English ground; and Eddie Paynter, who was lugged from a hospital bed with a temperature of 102 not out, to help England win the Bodyline Tour. So the professionals in Lancashire do not have it all their own way.

Club Cricket

This is played all over Britain. It is the backbone of the game and, possibly, of the entire socio-political structure of the country. It thus has much to answer for.

Club Cricket comes in three varieties:

1. **Suburban**. Very smart. Everyone wears white. Times, laws, customs are all scrupulously observed. Grounds are neatly kept, well-equipped and jealously guarded from all forms of building development. The cricket is as neat as cucumber sandwiches. There is an Annual Dinner (stag and a bit naughty) and an Annual Dance (mixed and not at all naughty).

2. **Village/Rural**. Not so smart, though a real attempt is made to provide adequate kit and equipment. The setting is idyllic, but since the ground has to serve so many other purposes (football, dog exercising, boot sales, village fête, etc.) the pitch will be 'sporting', and the outfield a mass of holes, bumps, nettles, cow pats and strange rural artefacts. The cricket is as lusty as the players.

3. **Municipal**. A very casual affair. Scratch teams play occasional games on grounds owned by the local council. Pitch and outfield are lethally rough. Nobody wears white, 'tea' consists of crates of lager and bags of doughnuts, there is an outstanding lack of skill. Exceptions to this are those towns with large immigrant populations where the cricket may be explosively entertaining.

Schools Cricket

State education has more or less given up cricket. It is expensive, needs a great deal of space, hours and hours of time, does not do a lot for hyperactive inner city youth, and is not likely to feature in any Core Curriculum imposed by the Secretary of State for Education.

So, schools cricket is left to the private sector. At Prep School, whole afternoons are given up to coaching: 'Bat and pad together, Tompkins Minor. I'm sure your father isn't paying three thousand a term to have you flashing at good length balls outside your off stump... What do you mean "it hurt"? It's a cricket ball, for goodness sake. It's supposed to hurt...'

At Public School, the coaching is intensified till the point is reached where the tyros play totally correctly and totally without effect.

Beach Cricket

The rules of Beach cricket are simple:

1. If the ball hits the breakwater post anywhere below the line scratched by Uncle Will, you're out.
2. You can't run more than 4 if the ball goes on the pebbles.
3. You can't expect Auntie Fay to bowl into the wind.
4. If you hit the ball into the sea, you go and get it.
5. Youngest bats first.
6. Strangers aren't invited to play without consulting Mum and Dad.
7. You can't run if Shep goes off with the ball.
8. Only ten more overs to be bowled after it's dark.

French Cricket

Nothing to do with the French, of course. The phrase comes from the Middle English 'frenesie criquet' (frensied cricket) – a suitable name for the non-stop, all action game where the main object is to break the batsman's leg.

The rules of French cricket are more complicated than those of Beach cricket, and vary enormously from area to area. Check local rules before you agree to play. These are some currently applicable in Catford.

1. Can't turn round if you didn't hit the ball.
2. First bounce one hand is 'out'.
3. Bowl from where the ball stops: no running forward with it.
4. Little Terry mustn't field too near.
5. Over the fence is 'out' and you have to go and ask.
6. Mustn't bowl too fast at Mrs Ruxley since her last operation.
7. Oldest bats first.
8. On the knee isn't out, unless the batsperson was deliberately crouching.
9. If anything happens to those delphiniums, that's the end of the game.

The World Cup

Having witnessed the commercial success of world cups in muddier sports, cricket now has its own.

It starts in a series of zonal matches throughout the world, and ends in a final knock-out competition. All games have to be one day, or one night contests. If they lasted any longer the World Cup would go on for ever. This would suit the tabloids, PR firms, airline executives and accountants but upset every true cricket fan.

STYLES OF CRICKET

While cricket fanatics are obsessively concerned with the minutiae of the game, the bluffer can afford to take a more general view, and make sweepingly grand statements. Don't bother with what length socks Mike Gatting wears, let your speciality be whole counties, nations, continents.

Nations

Every cricketing country exhibits a national style. The England team of today may look very different from that of 1859, but it is still essentially English in the way it plays cricket. It does not take long to discern each nations' traits.

England
Always ready to snatch defeat from the jaws of victory. Play without conviction or self-assurance*. Go out to bat as though they were the last line of defence for Western Civilisation. Rather embarrassingly tap each other on the bottom when they dismiss an opponent.

Batting:	Majestic. Brittle. Crisis prone.
Bowling:	England produce a good fast bowler once every 25 years. Next one due 2002.
Fielding:	Field like tigers, but usually in the wrong position.

West Indies
Lithe, lissom, spectacular. Capable of playing appallingly badly, but always with style and a broad smile of hostility on their lips. Go out to bat as if they had just woken up.

*I.T. Botham was an exception.

High fives whenever they dismiss or lame an opponent.

Batting: Glorious. Uninhibited.

Bowling: Very fast. Beautiful to watch. Dreadful
                 to face.

Fielding: Magnificent, unless they are losing.

Australia

Tough, uncompromising, joyless – unless they have just
hurt an opponent. Go out to bat like Ned Kelly entering
a Bank. Thump each other fiercely on the back when they
take a wicket, and then march menacingly towards the
surviving batsman.

Batting: They keep looking for another Bradman.
                 They probably won't find one.

Bowling: Hunt in pairs – Gregory & Macdonald,
                 Lindwall & Miller, Lillee & Thomson.

Fielding: Catch anything. Apt to go over the top.

New Zealand

Very young in spirit. Do remarkably well with such a
tiny population. All go out to bat wearing identical white
helmets so that it is impossible to tell one from another.
Maybe there are only three of them and they keep
taking it in turns.

Batting: Tend to rely on one or two 'class' players
                 e.g. Martin Crowe.

Bowling: All Kiwi bowlers are medium fast.
                 Opponents aren't dismissed, they succumb
                 to boredom.

Fielding: Awesomely keen.

South Africa

Never smile, even when they have hurt an opponent.
When things go right for them they go very, very right.
When things go wrong, it's a disaster. Rely on teamwork
rather than class players.

Batting:	The further down the order, the better the batsman.
Bowling:	Exciting when Donald bowls, dull when he doesn't.
Fielding:	Attempt to make up for shortcomings elsewhere by trying to run out one of their opponents every ball.

Pakistan

All have fierce moustaches which give their cricket a piratical air. Go out to bat as though looking for mischief. Polite smiles when they dismiss an opponent.

Batting:	Constantly finding gifted youngsters.
Bowling:	Keep alive the art of wrist spin bowling, for which they are to be deeply thanked.
Fielding:	Very good, when they take their hands out of their pockets in time.

India

Mysterious. Magical. Cricket literature is full of references to the mystical in Indian cricket, from Ranjitsinhji to the present. Play cricket as though there is no need to do anything else, and as if there is no such thing as time.

Batting:	Supple and subtle. Not much sledge hammer.
Bowling:	Supreme in spin – typical analyses: 103 overs 92 maidens 15 runs 1 wicket, or 12 overs 0 maidens 163 runs 8 wickets.
Fielding:	Often give the impression they are not interested in fielding.

Sri Lanka

Amazed the world by winning the 1995 World Cup, the equivalent of Merthyr Tydfil winning the FA Cup. Pioneered the system of sending in a 'pinch hitter' to open the innings in a one day game.

This is unfair because:

1. It's something you do in baseball, not cricket.
2. It's irreversibly successful when it works. Nothing is supposed to be irreversibly successful in cricket.

Zimbabwe
The latest to squeeze on to the international circuit. Achieved little or no success until they came to play England, when they won an entire series of one day games.

Cricketing Counties

Like the nations, English counties have individual styles. The following is a personal and prejudiced view, based on many happy hours of research in sun, wind and rain.

Derbyshire. Haven't won the Championship since 1936, though they have done better in one day games. Lack the grit of the north and the panache of the south.

Durham. The babes of first class cricket. Much derided when they first took the field in 1992, and tipped to come bottom in everything. One of the few English cricketing predictions to be almost accurate.

Essex. Not the force they were in the 1980s. Still keep dismissing opponents very cheaply at Chelmsford though, so still under suspicion.

Glamorgan. Always heroic, and heroically won the Championship in 1997. They do so every 20 or 30 years so it's best not to hold your breath for the next heroic success.

Gloucestershire. The county of Grace and Hammond. Have never won the Championship because they make a habit of gently letting someone else overtake them at the very end of the season. Polite but silly.

Hampshire. Arlott's county. Play with a West country accent. Very good at the one-day stuff. They nag their opponents out.

Kent. Did very well in the 1970s, but haven't done much since. Good record of playing home-grown cricketers, especially if they are called Cowdrey.

Lancashire. Dour. Gritty version of Derbyshire. Haven't won the Championship since 1934. Tend to approach four day matches as though they were six day matches.

Leicestershire. Also did well in the 1970s, and show signs of a bold revival. A county of passage for gifted cricketers and a haven for the almost-retired. Consists of players that no-one has ever heard of and Darren Maddy.

Middlesex. Very smart and swanky. Play almost all their matches at Lords. Have provided more England captains than is good for England or Middlesex. Favoured. Run up and down the Championship table like demented squirrels.

Northants. Another Midland county that has relied on imports. One was 'Nobby' Clark, a fast left-arm bowler who used to talk to birds flying overhead when he bowled. It takes all sorts.

Notts. Historically, one of the three great counties (the others are Surrey and Yorkshire). Bags of famous players – Larwood, Voce, the Hardstaffs, the Gunns and Arthur Shrewsbury – all of whom, sadly, are dead.

Somerset. Never won, never looked like winning the Championship, but has produced some wonderful players: Gimblett, Wellard, and (via Cheshire) Botham, all three of whom could hit the ball out of sight.

Surrey. Either fail to win a match till late June, or never win one after early July. Won the Championship seven years running in the 1950s. Players very smart and well creased. Crowd at the Oval very scruffy and well oiled, and rude to opponents.

Sussex. Used to be a great family affair, with brothers, cousins, fathers and sons all playing together. Have always kept an Eastern connection (Ranji, Duleep, Imran Khan, and now Amer Khan), but largely home-grown team.

Warwickshire. Their *annus mirabilis* of 1994 seemed proof of what should be an old cricketing adage: 'It's captains that win matches.' But Lara's theme very much in the minor key.

Worcestershire. The County badge is 'Shield Argent bearing Fess between Three pears Sable'. Tells you everything, doesn't it. Once called Fostershire because the family Foster practically made up the team. Has had some grandly named players: Root, Perks, Brain, Duff. Also one of the few famous umpires – Frank Chester.

Yorkshire. Always hoping to be on edge of grand renaissance since dropping Sir Geoffrey. Many great players: Rhodes (over 4,000 wickets), Sutcliffe, Leyland, Verity, Hutton and Hirst (the only person to score 2,000 runs and take 200 wickets in a season, and when asked if he thought anyone would ever equal his performance, replied 'Whoever does it will be tired'). Renaissance now a long time coming. Knives probably being sharpened behind the Committee Room door at this very moment.

TALKING ABOUT CRICKET

Sooner or later you will find yourself in the company of those who wish to show their great knowledge of cricket. They're all over the place – on trains, in pubs, at the seaside, at other sporting fixtures, even in doctor's waiting rooms. To put them in their place, all you need are a few names, a few facts, a confident air, and the merest hint that you can be every bit as MBB as they can.

Statistics

Statistics are what cricket is all about. Support comes from *Wisden* itself – which lists 120 different *headings* for cricket records, including:

— Record Hit
— Most Personal Boundaries in an Innings
— Sixteen or more Wickets in a Day
— Hundred in each innings and Five Wickets twice
— Highest Fourth Innings Totals
— Slowest Individual Test Batting
— Most Balls Bowled in a Test Match
— Most Consecutive Test Appearances
— Throwing the Cricket Ball

Wisden is often called the Cricketers' Bible. It is nothing like the Bible (except for its small print) containing no advice, no instructions, no moralising (well, not much), no gory or salacious passages and no Apocalyptic revelations (except when England lose). It is an Almanack, first published in 1864 by John Wisden, a small man who bowled fast, played for Sussex and England and took all ten wickets for the North against South at Lords in 1850.

Fortunately you do not have to know all 1250 pages. All you have to do to appear knowledgeable about cricket is to learn half a dozen facts of rare vintage and appreciation, that give you the ability to show off and shrug off every know-all with the sort of remark to which there is no reply.

Do not go for anything to do with Brian Lara. Every cricket buff in the world knows everything about Brian Lara. And don't go for the bizarre: Record Hit, Throwing the Cricket Ball, Wicket-Keeper' Hat Tricks, Victories without Losing a Wicket. Know-alls thrive on the bizarre. Go instead for such as the following:

a) The only player for the Combined Services to have scored a century on his debut in England – R. P. Hammond-Chambers-Borgnis, v New Zealanders at Portsmouth, 1937.

b) The last Englishman to score a hundred and take a hat-trick (three wickets in three successive balls) in the same match – R. E. S. Wyatt, for MCC v Ceylon, Colombo, 1926-7.

c) The last wicket-keeper to dismiss a hundred batsmen in a season – R. Booth of Worcestershire in 1964.

d) The fastest Test fifty – 28 minutes, by J. T. Brown, England v Australia, 1894-5.

e) The most balls bowled in a match – 917 by C. S. Nayudu for Holkar v Bombay 1944-5.

f) The Second oldest Test ground in England (most Know-alls are aware that The Oval is the oldest) – Old Trafford, ten days before Lords, in 1884.

Thus armed, you can contribute your share to the MBB statistical conversation that breaks out whenever rain stops play.

Names

1. Edward Budd (d. 1875). Great hitter, successful round arm bowler, and quick fielder. Suggest you open with: "Old Eddie Budd – always wanted to win the game off a single hit, as Lord Frederick Beauclerk used to say."

2. Robert Grimston (d. 1884) Suggest: "Old Bobby Grimston! Could not abide lawn-mowers! Wouldn't have them at Lords. And now there's all this fuss about pitches...!"

3. G. J. Bonner (d. 1912) Suggest: "Big hitting! You want to talk about big hitting! Bonner, that was the chap! Damn near killed Eddy Peate when he was caught and bowled once. Best innings was the ton he got for the Smokers v Non-Smokers at Lords, back in 1884."

4. J.T.B.D. Platts (f. 1870) Suggest: "Fast bowling! Batsmen today don't know the half of it! J. T. B. D. P.! There was a fast bowler. Hit George Summers on the cheekbone with a flyer. Poor old George died four days later. No helmets, you see. Quite right, too – load of nonsense."

5. T. Emmett (d. 1904) Suggest: "Skill! Dead! Gone! Lost art! You take a fast bowler like old Tom Emmett of Yorkshire. And he *was* fast. But his 'sostenuter' – pitched on leg and took the off bail. That's bowling!"

6 E. M. Grace (d. 1911) Suggest: "You all go on and on about W. G. Decent cricketer, certainly, but could he really hold a candle to E. M.?* And, of course, E. M. was the *older* brother. Taught W. G. all he knew. Sacrificed himself, you could say."

* None of the Grace family seems to have had a name, which is strange when you consider that they were a church-going family.

Here are a few more names to throw lightly into conversations, as you would chopped chives in a green salad.

Batsmen. Vijay Merchant ("wonderful cover drive"), Keith Miller ("pull shot like a cannon going off"), Andy Sandham ("what a judge of a run"), Harry Makepeace ("now, if ever there was an awkward sod to get out.")

Bowlers. Charlie Parker* ("talk about workload! There *was* a bowler"), Maurice Tate ("what an action! Not a wasted movement"), Bill Lockwood ("they could never, *never* spot his slower ball"), Tich Freeman ("no higher than the stumps and he terrified them all").

Fielders. Laurie Fishlock ("wonderful cover point"), John Langridge ("never missed anything in the slips"), Brian Statham ("fantastic arm. Threw the ball to the top of the stumps every time"), Edward Pooley ("three teeth knocked out by a cricket ball and he still caught eight and stumped four in a single match").

Odd Facts

1. Frederick Louis, Prince of Wales, died in the arms of his dancing master in 1751, the end caused by an internal abscess that had been long forming in consequence of a blow which he had received on the side from a cricket ball.

2. This could explain why royalty are careful cricketers. Edward VII made 0 for I Zingari v Norfolk. George V (when a young Midshipman) was demoted to HMS Bacchante's 2nd XI v HMS Cleopatra on Fiji in 1881.

* Not the one that played alto sax – he was a rotten bowler.

3. In Western Australia, two batsmen once scored 286 runs off a single hit, the ball lodging in a tall tree. The fielding side had to blow the ball out with a shotgun. NB: This means a) The two batsmen ran well over two miles each, wearing gloves and pads and carrying bats weighing a couple of kilos; b) The non-striker got nothing out of it; and c) The ball must have been extremely difficult to bowl with subsequently.

4. A sparrow was once struck and killed by a cricket ball at Lords. Its corpse, still embedded in the ball, is displayed in the museum there. Seagulls are made of sterner stuff. One, struck by a fearsome straight drive, was reverentially removed from the field of play but later recovered and flew off – behind the bowler's arm.

5. Virgin and Willey used to open the batting for Northants.

6. Terence Rattigan, playwright, was described by Wisden as 'an elegant stroke player, but unsound'.

7. Surrey Home Guard v Sussex Home Guard (Lords, 23rd July, 1942) had to be abandoned when one of the Surrey team, Andrew Ducat, died at the batting crease.

8. Although fanatics know all about the eight highest individual scores ever made in any kind of cricket, few recall that the tenth highest was by G. T. S. Stevens, at Neasden, in 1919.

9. In August 1855, the Second Royal Surrey Militia played Shillinglee and the whole team was disissed for 0, officers and all.

10. Nell Gwynn's great-grandson was an early member of the MCC, and the finest cricketer of his age.

Famous Cricketers

The exploits of Bradman, Hobbs, Hammond, Botham, Bedser, Sobers, Sutcliffe, Ranjitsinhji, Kapil Dev, Imran, Lindwall, Fry, Grace, Gunn, Verity, etc. are all to be found in dozens of books about cricket. Most of them have already been the subject of several biographies. The thing to do therefore, is have your own list of cricketers who were famous once upon a time, but who are hardly ever discussed today.

'Lumpy' Steven (1735-1829)

Herts, Kent and All England. A demon bowler, employed as a gardener by the fourth Earl of Sandwich (the cheese and pickle one), who appointed many great cricketers to his staff. Lumpy bowled fast and dangerously, downhill wherever possible – in those days the winner of the toss could choose the lie of the pitch. His worst afternoon was in 1775. Five Men of Kent needed one more wicket to beat Five Men of Hambledon. Several times Lumpy bowled 'through' the wicket, for these were the days of only two stumps. Lumpy's language is not recorded in *Wisden*.

John Small (1735-1826)

Hants and All England. The happy batsman who was at the crease when poor Lumpy was bowling that May afternoon in 1775. Small was a cheerful man who hung a sign outside his door which said:

> 'Here lives John Small
> Makes Bat and Ball,
> Pitch a wicket, Play at cricket
> With any man in England.'

You don't see signs like that nowadays.

David Harris of Hambledon
Poor fielder, much handicapped by gout. Had to sit in large armchair on field to rest after each ball was bowled.

Shock White
Famous for turning up one afternoon in Reigate, back in the 1770s, with a bat that was *wider than the wicket*. A good wheeze, but like most brilliant inventions it was immediately outlawed by a law specifically aimed so to do.

Brown of Brighton (1783-1857)
Sussex and England. Bowled underarm so fast that he killed a dog on the boundary.

F. William 'Nonpareil' Lillywhite (1792-1854)
Sussex. Not to be confused with Fred Lillywhite, the editor of *Fred's Guide*, William earned his nickname by the skill of his bowling. In 1831 he broke the record for the number of wickets taken in a season. One of the first Round Arm bowlers. Once took 14 wickets for South v North, but that was in an age when they sometimes played about a hundred and twenty a side. Still playing at 60, though he had to be carried to the wicket to bat.

Silver Billy Beldham (1766-1862)
Hambledon and Surrey. In many ways Silver Billy was a rogue. He bowled underarm grubs, sneaks, daisy cutters, or, when he did allow the ball to bounce, he stuck great lumps of sawdust on the side to make life extremely awkward for the batsman.

Master Ludd 19th century, but exact dates unknown.
A pragmatic cricketer, once struck on the foot by John Jackson of Notts. Ludd hobbled in agony. Jackson screamed his appeal. 'Not out,' said the umpire. 'Mebbe not,' said Master Ludd, 'but I'm a-goin'.' And he limped

away, presumably to continue his other career as machine wrecker in factories.

Fuller Pilch (1804-1870)

Norfolk and Kent. A professional in the days when professionals earned very little, usually had another occupation (Pilch was a tailor) and frequently went bankrupt. Pilch was a 'most famous player' who scored more runs than anyone else in cricket until W. G. Grace came along. To help him in this, and to make pitches play truer and faster, Pilch took his own scythe along and recut the grass before he batted.

Alfred Mynn (1807-1861)

Kent and All England. Like Pilch, Mynn was a pecunious professional, a hop merchant who occasionally went to prison for his inability to pay his creditors. Top hatted, six foot one, 20 stone, but graceful (so they say) in every movement. The first really great round arm fast bowler, so fast that opponents used specially heavy bats against him, more for protection than to score runs.

Mynn was an all-rounder, who opened the batting as well as the bowling, and became single wicket champion of All England in 1846, when he beat a violinist by an innings. Ten years earlier he had nearly lost a leg, severely damaged during a long innings – they did not wear pads in those days. Being too large for an inside seat, Mynn was strapped to the top of a stagecoach and carried all the way from Leicester to a surgeon in London, who, fortunately, decided against amputation.

Julius Caesar (1830-1878)

Rome, Surrey and All England. A little man from Godalming, said to be quick of eye and feet, and very fierce with his bat. A photograph of the English team to North America in 1859 shows Caesar with generous sideburns, a natty cap, a strong belt with metal clasp, and a deep coloured shirt. He looks more like an extra from a Chas 'n Dave commercial than a cricketer, though he does appear to be wearing a box for his photograph. Four years later, a photo of the English team to visit Australia 1863-4, shows Caesar in the same jaunty pose, the same belt, but now a striped shirt, no box (photography had improved enormously) and better fitting trousers.

Sir C. Aubrey 'Round-the-Corner' Smith
Cambridge University, Sussex, Transvaal and England. The nickname derived from his odd and angular run-up to the wicket when bowling. Captained England in his only Test in South Africa in 1888. Did well. Subsequently moved to Hollywood and became a movie actor. In this capacity he was about as good as you would expect most fast medium bowlers to be.

John Elicius Benedict Bernard Placid Quirk Carrington Dwyer
Sussex. The grandson of an Irish rebel chieftain who hailed from Australia. Another medium paced bowler, who probably did not get the fame he deserved as it was difficult to print the whole of his name on a scorecard.

H. A. 'Barmy' Gilbert
Worcestershire. A somewhat eccentric player, who had no cricket bag and used to arrive at grounds carrying his gear in his pockets.

G. H. Simpson-Hayward (1871-1936)
Worcestershire and England. The last great underarm 'lob' bowler. In 1909 he captained an MCC team on a tour of Egypt, usually bowling his lobs with the blazing desert sun behind him. Most of his opponents retired blind.

ATTENDING A MATCH

Impedimenta

In the days when Hambledon ruled, players wore breeches, silk shirts, stockings, buckled shoes, velvet caps with little tassles. Early heroes like William Beldham and William Lillywhite (the Non Pareil bowler) wore top hats. The first English team to tour Australia, in 1861-2, wore neckerchiefs and solid looking belts with brass buckles. At the beginning of the century, wicket keepers lined their gloves with slices of meat to give added protection to their hands.

Over the years much has changed. Fielders tore the nails from their fingers when they caught them in the buckles of their shoes. Top hats were not conducive to swift movement in the field. Little velvet caps did not keep the sun out of your eyes. More and more wicket-keepers became vegetarian and it's terribly difficult trying to catch a ball with your gloves full of lentils.

Pitches became harder, bowlers faster. Fashions changed. Fifty years ago, players wore heavy boots with massive spikes in the soles and heels. This enabled them to keep a firm grip on the ground, but it also slowed them down. Present day cricketers wear light shoes without spikes. This means they can move faster and spend more time in the air. In the 19th century, it was de rigueur to button the sleeves of your cricket shirt at the wrist. In the first half of the 20th century everyone rolled up their sleeves. Now, it doesn't seem to matter. What does matter is that players have adequate protection.

In top flight cricket, a batsman wears leg pads, thigh pads, arm pads, strong gloves, a helmet with visor and a box (see Glossary). Close fielders wear box and helmet. Much scorn is poured on cricketers who protect themselves by retired players."Old Tom/Jack/Reg/Rod," say the

Old Timers (all MBB) "never went in for this namby-pamby stuff, and he hooked bouncers right off his eyebrows." Then they toddle off to visit old Tom/Jack/Reg/Rod in the Home for the Incurably Crippled.

Grounds

Whatever the Hambledon Club may say, Broadha'penny Down is not the oldest ground in England. Nobody knows for sure which is, some claim Sevenoaks Vine, others the Artillery Ground in London, not many reckon the Warren Road Rec, Catford.

There are six sorts of cricket ground:

1. **International**. Used for Test matches. Huge. Biggest of all: Melbourne, Australia. Most famous: Lords, St Johns Wood, London. Most Oddly Named: The Gaddafi Stadium, Lahore, Pakistan. Most Beautiful: The Wanderers, Johannesburg, South Africa.

2. **County Urban**. Some counties play nearly all their matches on one ground: the Oval for Surrey, Lords for Middlesex. Others travel more widely, bringing cricket to the people (about ten people, usually). Yorkshire play at Headingley (Leeds), Sheffield, Bradford and Middlesborough. Kent play at Maidstone, Canterbury and Tunbridge Wells. Sussex play at Hove, Eastbourne, Horsham and Arundel. Glamorgan play at Cardiff, Swansea, Ebbw Vale, Pontyprydd and Abergavenny (which is miles from what used to be Glamorgan). But the major counties journey even further afield when they play minor counties, Scotland, or Ireland – to St Austell, Sleaford, Forfar, Eglinton and Jesmond. It's a glamorous life.

3. **County Rural**. There are some grounds where First Class cricket is played that have a reputation for beauty: Worcester, Bath, The Parks (Oxford), Fenners (Cambridge). But beauty is very much in the eye of the beholder, and each fanatic fights for his or her favourite. Some of us would even make a case for The Oval with its gasholder, municipal housing, lorries rattling up the Harleyford Road et al, though, sadly, no longer perfumed by the heady smells that once wafted from the Marmite factory at the Vauxhall end.

4. **Suburban**. Well kept. Level. Smart pavs. Securely fenced. Ample car parking. Reliable, but a little bit like Marks & Spencer's fashion, not very exciting.

5. **Rustic**. Lacking in care and respect. Interestingly undulating. Dreadful toilet facilities – you're better off in the woods. Sporting wickets. Well worth stopping to watch when you find one.

6. **Idyllic**. Mostly these exist in fiction, the imagination or history. Wittersham, Kent, looked good in 1845, Canterbury in 1760, and Mary-le-bone Fields in 1748. Swan Green, Lyndhurst looks pretty good today, and so does Southall Park, Bedfordshire. But some of us still fancy the Warren Road Rec, Catford.

Fans and Spectators

All you need to know historically about cricket fans is that there used to be two sorts: the Gents and the Plebs. The Gents wore suits or flannels and blazers and sat in the pavilion because they were members. They learnt by heart several phrases of appreciation and commendation: 'Well hit, sir!'/'Stroke, sir!'/'Fielded, sir!'/'Bowled, sir!'

The Plebs wore collarless shirts and baggy trousers and sat in the free seats. They also had a few stock phrases, none of which is printable.

Both Gents and Plebs came in their thousands to watch cricket. The Plebs barracked, but kept to their seats. At moments of uncontrollable excitement, the Gents cheered wheezily then shuffled off to the Gents.

Today there are two sorts of fans.

Elderly/Senile. Not necessarily aged, but betraying a mind that runs on very fixed rails down a not very long track. Somewhat grubby-looking, though may be sporting a pair of decent field glasses in a well-worn leather case. Thrives on sandwiches carefully packed at home and still uses a thermos.

Never rude, never drunk. Neatly and carefully fills in the scorecard. Spends the lunch and tea intervals quizzing neighbourly Seniles with general knowledge questions about Dates of Kings and Queens of England, British Prime Ministers and Cricket Statistics. Hurries home by bus or train immediately after close of play.

Young/Grossly Immature. May be well into his 30s or even 40s, but betraying a mind that has not yet grasped the basic principles of social intercourse. Dresses haphazardly, if at all, in bright shirts with palm-tree-and-sunset motifs, unbuttoned to the waist; low-slung jeans revealing buttock cleavage when bending down to pick up another can of McEwans; floppy brimmed hat worn in emulation of the cricketers he spends most of the afternoon verbally abusing. Never has binoculars. Rarely looks at the cricket – too busy smirking at his mates. Buys his food at the ground protesting vehemently at the price. Consumes can after can of lager, his eyes shrinking and his belly swelling with each can.

Always rude. Always drunk. Doesn't fill in the scorecard (can't write) but rolls it into a megaphone through which to hurl his pearls of wit at all and sundry. Spends the lunch and tea intervals falling down. Looks round desperately, for a source of more lager at close of play.

Essential Supplies

Unless you fall into the youthful category above, you need to prepare yourself carefully for an outing to a cricket match. The following list is not exhaustive, but should go some way to making the day less arduous than it might otherwise be:

1. Overcoat, possibly two.
2. Raincoat.
3. Large umbrella.
4. Flask of: a) Brandy – to combat hypothermia; b) tea.
5. Folding chair (or see 12).
6. Gumboots.
7. Vast amount of food.
8. Selection of waterproof games to play when it rains.
9. Copy of *Wisden*, to refute false statements of those around you.
10. Exercise book, in case some poor cricketer mooches over hoping somebody will ask for his autograph.
11. Insect repellent – just in case the sun and the mosquitoes come out.
12. Soft cushion – only Rugby League seats are harder than cricket seats.
13. Sugar – many cricket grounds serve French mustard in identical catering packs to those with sugar. French Mustard makes a poor substitute sweetener for a plastic cup of tea.
14. Burn cream and plasters for when the plastic cup cracks and sends scalding tea down your arm.

15. Sunglasses – there may be someone you want to avoid.
16. Daily or local paper with list of What's On at the Cinema, so you'll know where to go when play is cancelled for the day at 3 pm.

Things to Say at Cricket Matches

If the batsman is doing well:
1. "It's all in the timing."
2. "It's all in the wrists."
3. "It's all in the footwork."
4. "It's all in the left shoulder."
5. "Shades of the great George." (Chances are those around you won't know if you mean Hurst, Gunn, Tydesley, Formby or Gershwin.)

If the batsman is doing badly:
1. "Look where s/he's standing!"
2. "Look where his/her front foot goes!"
3. "Look at the left shoulder!"
4. "Look at the backlift!"
5. "Just letting the ball hit the bat!"

If the bowler is doing well:
1. "It's all in the run-up."
2. "It's all in the left shoulder."
3. "It's all in the body pivot."
4. (Appreciatively) "It's all a question of line and length".
5. "Shades of the great George." (Those around won't know if you mean Lohmann, Geary, Simpson-Hayward, Macaulay or Harrison.)

If the bowler is doing badly:
1. "Look at the action!"

2. "Look at the left shoulder!"
3. "Bowling round (or over) the wicket to a left (or right) hander! On this pitch! Cuh!"
4. "Look at the field that's been set! Doesn't know where to pitch 'em!"
5. (Exasperatedly) "It's all a question of line and length".

If the fielders are doing well:
1. "It's all a question of fitness."
2. "It's all a question of fielders winning matches."
3. "All you need to do – keep the head still."
4. "What a throw! It's all in the left shoulder!"
5. "Shades of the great George." (It could be anybody.)

If the fielders are doing badly:
1. "It's all a question of concentration/anticipation/keeping your eye on the ball."
2. "It's all a question of being on your toes/walking in as the bowler runs up to bowl/keeping fit."
3. "The ball was past before he took his hands out of his pockets."
4. "Worth 40 runs to the other side!"
5. "They'll have a job hiding him/her in the field..."

If the wicket keeper is doing well:
1. "Shades of the great George." (Everyone should know you mean Duckworth.)

Things Not to Say at Matches

1. Anything about 'backstop'.
2. Anything about 'the hitter'.
3. Anything crude – unless you are surrounded by people doing likewise.

4. Uncouth terms such as: 'Tonk it!'/'Bowl at his head!'/'Bet you drop it! Yah! See!'
5. Anything that suggests you haven't a clue as to what is going on. Those around you will immediately seek to explain, and that's even more MBB than cricket.

Things Not to Do at Matches

There is one capital offence at any cricket match, and that is *to move behind the bowler while he is bowling*.

This is not easy because:

a) most cricket grounds have the pavilion directly behind the bowler's arm.
b) the pavilions are where members sit.
c) members are usually old and need to stretch their legs from time to time, often at very short notice.
d) cricket matches last a long time, and you can buy drink all day.

There is, therefore, considerable moving about behind the bowler's arm, but this doesn't excuse you. It is still conduct beneath contempt. If guilty, best join the Foreign Legion. They don't play cricket: not even French.

Weather

Rain doesn't always stop play. Club cricket often continues in the most appalling conditions. This is because club cricket doesn't matter. Professional cricket (which does matter) stops immediately, and there is an unseemly rush for the pavilion by players and umpires alike.

Eventually, the rain stops. Umbrellas are folded. Macs

are shaken. Spectators squint up at the sky. After decades of disappointment, the spark of optimism has still not died. 'Brighter over there,' you will hear them say. Or: 'Fine drying wind, shouldn't take long.' These are the very stuff of old England, the sort who, huddled in a tent on the way back from the South pole, would have turned to Captain Scott and said: 'It's turned out nice again.'

Beware of querying why the cricket season always starts in April (the wettest month of the year), and why more use isn't made of September (much drier and warmer). Remember that any change in cricket is likely to interfere with some obscure record – in this case that of a batsman scoring A Thousand Runs in May (in reality 'before the end of May'). Only two people have done this in the last 50 years, but fanatics live in hope.

The other major cause of loss of play is bad light, especially towards the end of a day's play. Well over half the number of games played ending up as 'drawn' because they run out of time. This is because cricket ends so late (6.30 or 7 pm) which in turn is because cricket starts so late (11 or 11.30 am). State firmly that it has probably got something to do with: a) the Stock Exchange; and b) the time it took for a hansom meeting the 9.20 from Winchester to get to St John's Wood in 1855.

If none of these gambits is suitable, you can always fall back on one certain effect of wet weather on cricket: that it gives counties in the eastern half of England an unfair advantage. The eastern half is drier, which means that more matches can be played to a finish. This is why eastern counties win the Championship more often than those in the west – almost twice as often, in fact.

HISTORY

The important thing to remember is that the whole of
cricket is History, most of it intricate and unimportant,
much of it ill-recorded and unmemorable – what more
could the honest bluffer ask for? Every facet of the game
has its history. Nobody knows it all. Memorise the
following list and you will be more than halfway to being
the scourge of every pavilion, Long Room and bar from
here to the MCG (familiar way of referring to the
Melbourne Cricket Ground).

1666   First reference to a cricket club – St Albans.

1709   First county match – Kent v Surrey.

1774   First Laws of Cricket drafted. Some nobs and
       gents met in the Star and Garter, Pall Mall, and
       drafted laws that cover the basic game still today.
       Before falling to the floor, awash with claret, they
       drew up rules covering the size of bat, weight of
       ball, number of stumps, how dismissals could
       occur, duties of umpires, etc. They also attempted
       to regulate betting, which was prodigious on
       cricket matches (and everything else – in 1757 you
       could get four to one on George II being killed in
       battle). Their one law that has not survived was
       that visiting teams could choose the location of the
       pitch.

1782   White Conduit Club (WCC), gents only, forerun-
       ner of the MCC, formed.

1787   The WCC became the MCC (Marylebone Cricket
       Club), by turning their first initial upside down.

1787   Thomas Lord (of Lord's fame) built his first cricket
       ground in Dorset Square.

1789 First English tour planned. Unfortunately, the destination was Paris, and the tour was cancelled when the French Revolution broke out. It seems typical of the French to get their priorities so absurdly wrong.

1811 Thomas Lord opened his second cricket ground, the lease on the first having expired.

1813 Parliament decided to cut a canal through Lord's second cricket ground. Lord moved it to St John's Wood, where Lords has remained.

1836 First County club formed – Sussex ground.

1844 First International Match – Canada v USA.

1859 First overseas tour. An English team visited Canada and the USA. The Americans very sensibly postponed their Civil War for three years to allow this tour to proceed.

1861 First English tour of Australia. This included a Single Wicket match (see Glossary) between Mr Griffiths and eleven assorted Aussies. The Aussies failed to make a single run between them, and then bowled a wide at Mr Griffiths, thus immediately losing the match. It is best to keep quiet about this late on a Saturday night in the Earls Court Road or any other part of Australia.

1864 Overarm bowling legalised. Until then, bowling had been 'under' or 'round' arm. Women were the first to stop bowling underarm as they nearly broke their wrists on their crinolines.

1877 First Test Match – Australia v England.

The Golden Age

Cricket has had several Golden Ages and each one
would seem to precede a major war, so it is to be hoped
that there will be no more.

In the early days, cricket matches were ramshackle
affairs with bizarre scratch sides: Middlesex with Two of
Berkshire and One of Kent v Essex with Two more
Given; Five of the Globe Club v Four of the MCC; The
Original English Lady Cricketers, elegantly and appro-
priately attired v Similar; Twenty Three of Kent v
Thirteen of England; and A One Legged XI v A One
Armed XI – of which it was reported: 'The men with
one leg beat the one-arms by one hundred and three
runnings. After the match was finished, the eleven one-
legged men ran one hundred yards for twenty guineas.
The three first divided the money.'

First Golden Age (1848-1882)

Bathed in a sea of nostalgia, the First Golden Age is
captured in poetry. It was the time of Newbolt's:

'There's a breathless hush in the Close tonight...'

and Francis Thompson's:

'For the field is full of shades as I near the shadowy coast,
And a ghostly batsman plays to the bowling of a ghost,
And I look through my tears on the soundless-clapping
   host,
As the run stealers flicker to and fro,
To and fro:-
O my Hornby and my Barlow long ago!'

Like all Golden Ages, it was a time of great batsmen,
but was brought to an end by a demon bowler – the

mighty Spofforth. He wrecked Grace's MCC side at Lords, taking six wickets for four runs in 23 balls, and then 'killed' English cricket at The Oval. England only needed thirty four runs to win, with eight wickets left (including that of Grace), when Spofforth is reported to have said: 'Boys, it can be done.' He promptly took seven wickets, and Australia won by seven runs. There followed agrarian outrages in Ireland, war in Egypt and the Sudan, riots in Burma, the collapse of Gladstone's government and the end of the First Golden Age.

Second Golden Age (1899-1914)

A plethora of great batsmen: Hobbs, Hayward, Abel, Maclaren, Ranji, Trumper, Armstrong and Wilfred Rhodes. C.B. Fry was regarded as the most glamorous figure of the Second Golden Age until a jolly unsporting biography revealed what he was up to besides playing cricket and football for England, gaining a First at Oxford, going as a delegate to the League of Nations, breaking the World Long Jump record and being invited to be King of Albania.

Then there was Gilbert 'the Croucher' Jessop, who scored two of the fastest centuries ever (perhaps *the* fastest ever when it is taken into account that hits over the ropes counted only four runs in Jessop's time), Frank Woolley (reckoned the most graceful cricketer ever), Albert Trott (the only man to hit a ball over the pavilion at Lords), and the Hon. F.S. Jackson (who managed to play cricket with his sleeves rolled down *but not buttoned at the wrist*).

There were also a few great and long-suffering bowlers. The best of them, Tom Richardson, who bowled fast all day at The Oval, would pack his bag at close of play and walk 12 miles home, stopping, it is said, at every pub along the way.

By 1914 Spofforth was 61 and too old to demolish the Second Golden Age, so the Kaiser (right hand cowshot bat and poor close to wicket fielder) intervened instead.

Third Golden Age (1930-9)

This was again a time of long hot summers, easy wickets and great batsmen. Far more triple centuries were scored in the 1930s than any other decade. Among the giants were Bradman, Sutcliffe, Hammond, McCabe, Headley, Ponsford, Duleepsinhji (Ranji's nephew) and a very young Hutton. There were also a few who hung on from the Second Golden Age, among them Woolley, Hobbs and Rhodes, who, at the age of 52½, bowled 45 overs for 39 runs against the West Indies, a feat unlikely to be repeated.

The Third Golden Age came to an end on 1st September, 1939 – when Hedley Verity took seven wickets for nine runs in six overs at Hove, and Hitler (who never played the game) invaded Poland.

GLOSSARY

Beamer – A fast, potentially lethal ball that flies straight at the batsman's head. Bowlers always pretend they didn't mean to.

Benefit – A reward given to old lags who have performed faithfully for their club. Fund raising activities include special 'celebrity' matches with Show Biz XIs, dinner/dances, collection boxes passed round grounds. The poor old lag then has to justify the money that has been collected.

Blue – A name given to University players because they start the season earlier than other players and so suffer more from cold.

Box – A metal or plastic codpiece worn by all batsmen, nervous fielders and forgetful bowlers.

Bumper – A fast, potentially lethal ball that bounces just in front of the bowler and then rises towards the batsman's head. Bowlers always pretend that they did mean to.

Cowshot – A scything blow which has little chance of making contact, but is very exciting if it does. The name has a scathing, rural connotation.

Cut – A sophisticated attempt to hit the ball once it is passed you but before it has reached the wicket-keeper's hands, otherwise there is the terrible noise of knuckles splintering.

Dolly – Supposedly, a very easy catch. Anyone who has ever played cricket will tell you that there is no such thing.

Declaration – A means by which the batting side bring their innings to a premature close, showing off, and hinting they have already scored more runs than they will need.

Follow-on – A means by which the fielding side shows off, making their opponents bat again because they have scored so few runs.

Full toss ('Full bunger' coll.) – A ball which fails to bounce before it reaches the batsman. Very easy to hit, therefore, since it is not subject to the vagaries of the pitch or the wiles of the bowler's spin. Usually ends up in the Squire's duckpond.

Googly – An offbreak (q.v.) bowled with a leg break (q.v.) action. Sometimes called a Bosie, because Lord Alfred Douglas was similarly deceptive. A left hander's version of a googly is called a Chinaman.

Hall volley – Military salute fired by an army too poor to afford enough rounds of ammunition. Also a ball which lands just in front of the batsman.

Hoick – Noise made by cricketer about to expectorate. Also cowshot.

In – A word you do *not* shout when you reach the safety of the other end of the pitch having made a run.

Leg/On side – That side of the field your bum points to when you are batting.

Leg bream – A ball that starts on your bum side and then heads towards to the off side (q.v.).

Long hop – A ball which lands appetisingly way in front of the batsman, giving plenty of time to roll up the sleeves, spit on the hands (see Hoick) and tonk it to the boundary.

Made a run – A phrase you never use. The correct description is 'scored a run'.

Maiden – Six balls in succession by the same bowler without a run being scored: i.e. a phenomenon without blemish.

Nightwatchman – A poor batsman who is sent in late at night when the light is bad, wickets are falling and the bowler and fielders are rampant with success, to protect much better batsmen. Some of us feel that our whole way of life is founded on similar principles.

Notts Trots (also Surrey Hurries and Delhi Belly) – Uproariously humorous term given by cricketers to the runs that have nothing to do with cricket.

On/Off side – That side of the field that your nose points to when batting.

Offbreak – A ball that starts on your nose side and turns to hit you in the box.

Out – A word you do *not* shout when one of the other side is dismissed.

Over-rate – a) The number of overs bowled in an hour. b) What the press do to any young English cricketer who scores more than 10 against Australia or the West Indies.

Pull – Hitting a ball from the nose to the bum side.

Seam – The part of the cricket ball where they sew it together.

Seamers – Making the ball swerve from one side to another by altering the angle of the seam through the air. Very clever stuff.

Selectors – Formerly a group of toffs who chose the England team, now more likely to be swanky ex-pros.

Sighters – A term which seeks to excuse bowling a load

of tripe that goes in all directions save at the stumps.

Sightscreen – White painted boards, often on little wheels, which are placed on the boundary behind the bowler's arm so that members in the pavilion cannot see what is going on: i.e. the cricket is screened from their sight.

Single wicket cricket – Ancient form of the game recently revived. A sort of gladiatorial contest where one-person teams compete for prize money, usually in a park in Hong Kong.

Surrey Cut – Name given to a flashing and flamboyant stroke that seeks to send the ball nose side, but instead snicks it between the batsman's legs to the bum side. Often profitable, but never graceful.

Taverner – Name given to someone too poor or too yobbish to be a Full Member of a cricket club, but who has alcoholic aspirations.

Tonk – A mighty and primitive blow at the ball.

Yorker – A ball which pitches either a) on your foot, severely injuring and/or dismissing you LBW; or b) just underneath your bat, squeezing through and bowling you; or c) right on the bottom of your bat, sending shock waves up and down both arms, and giving you the feeling that you have spent the last six hours wrestling with a pneumatic drill. Called 'Yorker' because a Lancashire player was the first to master the skill.

THE AUTHOR

Born in 1938 Nick Yapp still plays cricket regularly (once a year at the Warren Road Rec.) in the Annual Political Cricket Match for the Oswald Mosley Cup.

A hurried, anxious bat whose highest score is 84 for Cheam 3rd XI, he has never fulfilled the potential that early days on the beach at Worthing suggested. His slow, tripe bowling, however, had been popular with batspersons all over South London, and he still manages to look hawkish in the field unless the ball comes too near him. He can keep a neat scorebook but is frightened of umpiring.

His earliest cricketing memories are of playing in the back garden, where he and his older brother would pretend to be whole county sides (never Middlesex) and inflict a good deal of damage to the close boarded fence and Mr Smith's rockery next door (serve him right – he never threw the ball back).

A schoolboy member at The Oval in the days when Surrey won the Championship seven years in a row, he remains a devoted Surrey fan. He still cannot bear to see them lose.

He has his own bat, pads and gloves, and is open to offers.

THE BLUFFER'S GUIDES®

Available at £2.99:

Accountancy	Personal Finance
The Classics	Philosophy
Computers	Public Speaking
Consultancy	The Quantum Universe
Cricket	The Rock Business
Doctoring	Rugby
Economics	Science
The EU	Seduction
The Flight Deck	Sex
Golf	Skiing
The Internet	Small Business
Jazz	Stocks & Shares
Law	Tax
Management	Teaching
Marketing	University
Men	Whisky
Music	Wine
Opera	Women